GOTCHA GADGETS

BY
BEN GROSSBLATT
**& THE SCIENTISTS
OF KLUTZ LABS**

KLUTZ®

creates activity books and other great stuff for kids ages 3 to 103. We began our corporate life in 1977 in a garage we shared with a Chevrolet Impala. Although we've outgrown that first office, Klutz galactic headquarters remains in Palo Alto, California, and we're still staffed entirely by real human beings. For those of you who collect mission statements, here's ours:

- *CREATE WONDERFUL THINGS*   • *BE GOOD*   • *HAVE FUN*

Write Us
We would love to hear your comments regarding this or any of our books.
We have many!

KLUTZ.
450 Lambert Avenue
Palo Alto, CA 94306
thefolks@klutz.com

Manufactured and printed in China. 84

Distributed in the UK by
Scholastic UK Ltd
Westfield Road
Southam, Warwickshire
England CV47 0RA

Distributed in Australia by
Scholastic Australia Ltd
PO Box 579
Gosford, NSW
Australia 2250

Distributed in Canada by
Scholastic Canada Ltd
604 King Street West
Toronto, Ontario
Canada M5V 1E1

Produced by becker&mayer!
Bellevue, Washington
11951

ISBN 978-0-545-44933-5

4 1 5 8 5 7 0 8 8 8

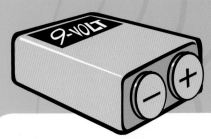

- Rechargeable batteries are only to be charged under adult supervision.
- Rechargeable batteries are to be removed from the toy before being charged.

INSTRUCTIONS FOR PARENTS

- Warning: Only for use by children aged 8 years and older.
- To ensure proper safety and operation, battery replacement must always be done by an adult.
- Use only 9-volt batteries.
- Hook up the battery with the correct polarity.
- Keep all batteries away from small children, and immediately dispose of any depleted batteries safely.
- Always remove depleted batteries from the toy.
- Do not short-circuit the supply terminals.
- The battery will overheat if short-circuited.
- If your projects aren't working, replace the battery with a new 9-volt battery.
- Do not recharge non-rechargeable batteries.
- Do not use a battery if it is leaking or abnormal in any way.
- Do not disassemble the battery or put it in an open flame.
- Possible leakage of electrolyte if battery is abused.

ELECTRICITY MEETS IMMATURITY

Thousands of scientists and engineers worked over the course of hundreds of years to develop the materials that come with this book. Thanks to their dedication, you can learn about circuits, build your own electronic gadgets — and annoy your family and friends like no one has ever been annoyed before.

THE GADGETS

LIGHT SENSOR

SITS IN THE DARK, WAITING PATIENTLY FOR THE CHANCE TO SCARE YOUR LITTLE BROTHER

PUSH BUTTON

AN ALL-PURPOSE SOUND-EFFECTS MACHINE THAT MARKS LIFE'S GREAT (AND NOT SO GREAT) MOMENTS

MOTION SENSOR

LETS YOU KNOW WHEN SOMEONE MAKES THE WRONG MOVE

DOOR ALARM

LETS YOU KNOW WHEN SOMETHING IS REALLY AND TRULY ALARMING

WHAT YOU GET

With the stuff in this book, you can build gadgets and use them to set traps, play games, and trick your friends and family. Our ideas will get you started, but once you understand how these gizmos work, you'll think of better ones.

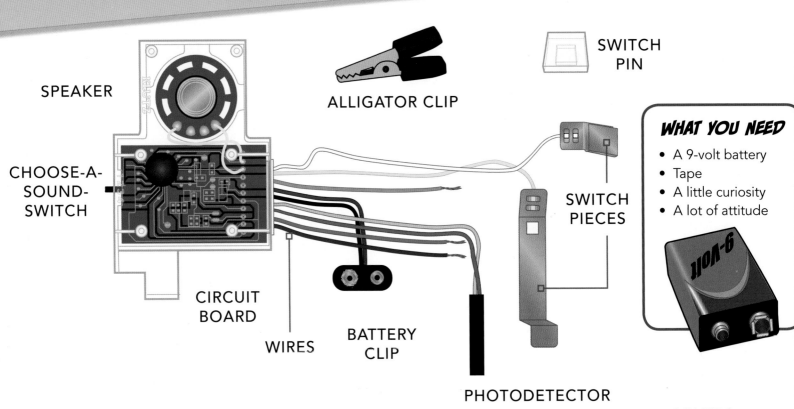

SPEAKER

ALLIGATOR CLIP

SWITCH PIN

CHOOSE-A-SOUND-SWITCH

SWITCH PIECES

WHAT YOU NEED

- A 9-volt battery
- Tape
- A little curiosity
- A lot of attitude

CIRCUIT BOARD

WIRES

BATTERY CLIP

PHOTODETECTOR

COVERS

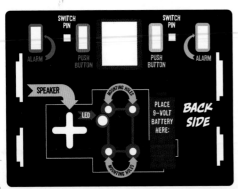

GADGET DOCK

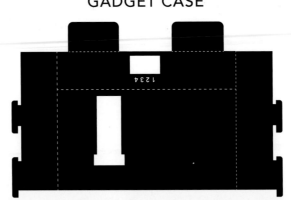

GADGET CASE

BUILD YOUR BASIC GADGET

1. Make a loop from a 1-inch (2.5-cm) piece of tape. Stick it to the bottom of the circuit board in the middle of the four pegs. Line up the red LED with the red hole in the dock and push the pegs into the green holes.

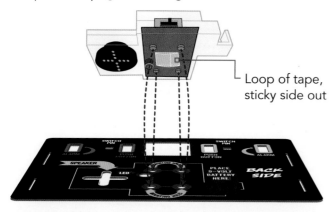

Loop of tape, sticky side out

2. Slide the lower "leg" of the short metal switch piece into the green alarm slot so the cardboard of the dock is pinched between the upper and lower legs.

BATTERY TIPS

- When you hook up the battery, electricity moves through your gadget. If you know you won't be using your gadget for a few days, unhook the battery to avoid draining it.
- Never connect the plus side of the battery directly to the minus side. That will drain your battery in a hurry.
- Not all batteries are the same size. If your battery slips out of the holder, put a loop of tape (see step 1 above) between the holder and the battery.

The stuff in this book can be wired to make four different gadgets. Follow these instructions to put together the basic gadget. Then we'll show you how to connect wires to make it into a light sensor, a motion sensor, a door alarm, and a sound-effects machine.

3. Place the large metal switch piece across the big square hole, as shown. You may have to push some wires out of the way. Press the switch pin through the square holes in the switch and the dock to hold the switch in place.

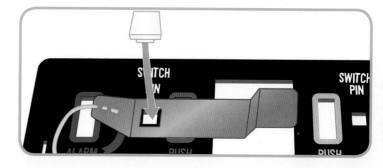

4. Press the battery clip onto the terminals of a 9-volt battery. Insert the battery into the battery holder as shown. Make sure the terminals point in the same way as the picture on the dock.

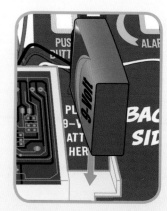

Your basic gadget is ready for action. Electricity is flowing, but you haven't given it anything to do just yet.

FUNNY SOUNDS

Transform your basic gadget from a quiet piece of electronic potential into an annoying noise machine.

1. Move the choose-a-sound switch on the side of the circuit board to number 1.

2. Find the orange wire and the green wire and gently twist the metal ends of the wires together. Clip the twisted wires with the alligator clip so they stay together. Make sure no other metal wire ends or switch pieces are touching.

3. Cover the end of the photodetector with your finger. Take your finger away and your gadget will reward you with wild applause. Your gadget is now a light sensor, reacting with sound when the photodetector is hit with light.

4. Use the choose-a-sound switch to try all the sounds.

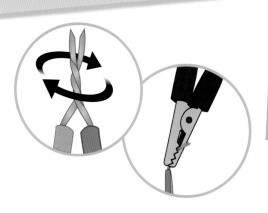

YOUR FINGER HERE

TWISTY TIP
You'll be connecting and disconnecting wires to make different gadgets. So don't twist the wires too tight.

Don't be alarmed if your gadget screams (or makes some other sound) while you are wiring it or moving it.

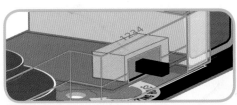

SOUND EFFECTS:

1. WILD APPLAUSE
2. SOMETHING UNMENTIONABLE
3. SAD TROMBONE (WAH, WAH, WAH, WAH)
4. BLOOD-CURDLING SCREAM

SCREAM! APPLAUSE! SAD TROMBONE! UNMENTIONABLE!

6

SERIOUS SCIENCE

In the wires of your gadget, tiny particles are on the move. These particles, called **electrons**, are way too small for you to see. A bunch of electrons, all moving in the same direction, make an **electric current**.

To understand invisible things, scientists sometimes compare them to everyday stuff that you can see. Think of an electric current as cars traveling on a one-way street.

Why one-way traffic? Because electrons always flow from the negative terminal to the positive one.

Using cars as electrons, this picture shows what's happening in a very simple electric setup—just a current flowing from a battery, through a light bulb, and back to the battery.

Battery = Gas Station
The movement of electrons starts and ends at the battery. That circular path is known as an electric circuit. The battery is like a gas station—it provides the power that makes the electrons move. Cars always return to the gas station, and electrons in this circuit always return to the battery.

Wires = Roads
Like cars, electrons move only when they have somewhere to go. Cars travel on roads; electrons in this circuit travel through metal wires. When the electric current flows through the light bulb, it glows.

WHAT DOES THIS HAVE TO DO WITH MY GADGET?

In your gadget, you make a road for electrons when you put in the battery and twist wires together. The circuit board sends the electric current through different parts of the gadget, depending on how you connect the wires. When that current flows through the speaker, your gadget makes a sound.

WHAT DO I DO IF MY GADGET DOESN'T WORK?

Your wires must have a good metal-to-metal connection for electricity to flow through your gadget. Electricity flows through metal — but it can't flow through the plastic that coats the wires. Check the wires that you've twisted together. Make sure that the metal of one wire wraps around the metal of the other wire, and that the clip touches the metal of both wires. If that doesn't work, try disconnecting the battery and then reconnecting it (or try a new battery). Don't worry about shocking yourself. The 9-volt battery doesn't put out enough power to shock you.

HOW DO I MAKE THIS MESS OF WIRES LOOK BETTER?

We've provided a handy cardboard case. Here's how to put it together:

1. Lay the case on a table, white side up. Bend up and crease on all the fold lines to make a box, as shown.

2. Set the case on the table so it's resting on the bottom — the end with a rectangular hole. Fold the flaps on the bottom inside. Position the dock as shown and slide the tabs on the case through the slots in the dock. You may need to move the short switch piece slightly to get the tab in place. The flaps will end up tucked under the battery and the circuit board. You can see the battery and reach the choose-a-sound switch through the holes in the case. The project wires should stick out the top of the case.

3. Push the tabs toward the outside edges of the dock to lock them in place.

TWISTY TIP

If you want to make a circuit more permanent, you can tape the wires together instead of using the alligator clip.

1. Twist together the metal ends of the two wires. Gently pull the wires to make sure they will not come apart.

2. Bend the twisted wires and wrap a 1-inch (2.5-cm) piece of regular or masking tape around all the exposed metal.

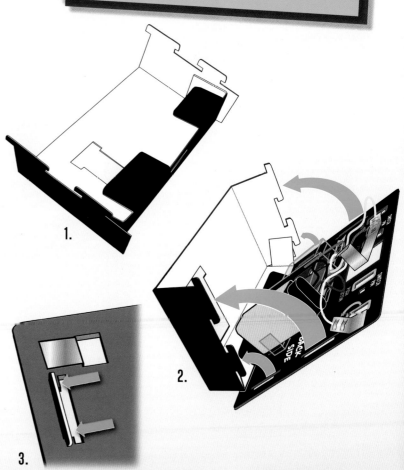

1.

2.

3.

HOW DO I ADD A COVER TO THE CASE?

You'll find an assortment of covers in the same box where you found the gadget dock and case.

1. Lay the case on a table with the tabs pointing up. Gently press the cover onto the dock so the tabs poke through the slits. It will be a tight fit, so be careful not to tear the cover.

2. Once the tabs are in place, slide the cover under the hooks on the tabs. When you're done, the bottom edge of the cover and the bottom edge of the dock should line up.

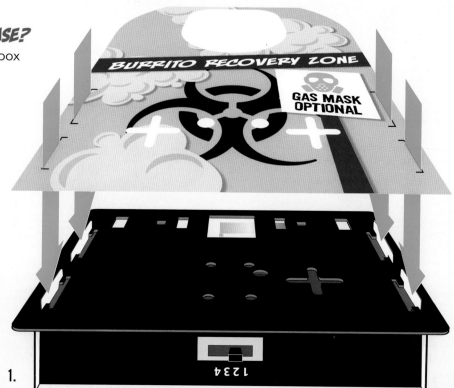

1.

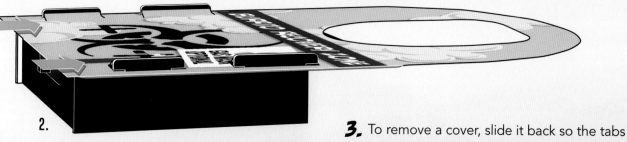

2.

3. To remove a cover, slide it back so the tabs can go through the slits. Then carefully pull out each tab separately.

NOW WHAT?

Turn the page to find out what you can do with your gadget.

LIGHT SENSOR

The gadget that waits in the dark

If your gadget is a highway for electricity, the photodetector is a traffic light.

When the light is on, the current flows.

DO THIS FIRST

1. Build your basic gadget (page 5) and wire it so it works as a light sensor (page 6).

2. Test it by putting your finger over the photodetector to block the light. When you take your finger off the photodetector, the current flows and the speaker makes a sound.

YOUR FINGER HERE

WHAT'S GOING ON?

When the photodetector is in the dark, it blocks the flow of electric current through your gadget. When it's in the light, it lets the current flow, triggering a sound. Turn off the light and the gadget resets so it's ready to make another sound. Lights on, **GOTCHA!**

Darkness turns the traffic light red — no current flows.

PARDON YOU!

SOUND SETTING: *UNMENTIONABLE*

Hide your light sensor behind a tissue box or other object in the bathroom. When someone turns on the light in the middle of the night, the unmentionable sound will, um, announce their presence.

TOTAL REMOTE CONTROL

SOUND SETTING: *UNMENTIONABLE*

Turn on the TV and select your favorite channel. Place your gadget on the sofa and hide it behind a pillow. Extend the photodetector wire and set the remote directly on top of it. *Make sure no light is hitting the photodetector.* If any would-be channel-changers dare to pick up the remote, they will learn a valuable (and embarrassing) lesson.

WHO TURNED ON THE LIGHT?

To catch a snoop, stash your light sensor in a closed box or bag or drawer. When someone lets in the light, they set off the sound. This basic trick is the electronic equivalent of a springy snake coiled up in a fake can of nuts.

PROTECT THE COOKIES
SOUND SETTING: *SAD TROMBONE*

Put the light sensor in a cookie jar. Tell your family that you've made a batch of delicious cookies that must "cure" in total darkness for 12 hours. How long before a hungry sneak lifts the lid?

SNARE-A-SNOOP
SOUND SETTING: *APPLAUSE*

Place the light sensor in a drawer along with a note that says, "Congratulations! You are the world's biggest snoop!" Close the drawer and hide nearby.

FOIL LATE-NIGHT FRIDGE RAIDS
SOUND SETTING: *SCREAM*

Right before bedtime, place the light sensor inside the fridge. When a midnight snacker opens the door, the refrigerator will scream. Race to the kitchen and catch the nibbler in the act. (If you're a heavy sleeper, don't be surprised if you find your gadget in the trash the next morning.)

BOX OF WHAT?
SOUND SETTING: *UNMENTIONABLE*

Put the light sensor in a box labeled "Toxic Gas." Need we say more?

POINTERS FOR PRANKSTERS

- THESE TRAPS WORK BEST NEAR A BRIGHT LIGHT.

- WHEN YOU SET YOUR TRAP, MAKE SURE THE PHOTODETECTOR ISN'T BLOCKED OR COVERED BY ANYTHING.

- TAPE THE PHOTODETECTOR IN PLACE TO MAKE SURE IT STAYS NEAR THE OPENING OF THE TRAP WHERE THE LIGHT WILL HIT IT.

- TO MAKE SURE YOUR TRAP WORKS, ALWAYS TEST IT A FEW TIMES.

LIGHT SENSOR
SCREAM MACHINES

Show your friends how much you care by scaring them half to death.

FRIGHT BRIGHT

SOUND SETTING: *SCREAM*

THE SETUP

This one is great for a campout or a slumber party. Before dark, untwist the wires and move them apart so they aren't touching (you don't want your gadget to scream until you're ready). Hide your gadget somewhere out of sight with the photodetector positioned where you can hit it with your flashlight beam. When everything's dark and no one's paying attention, twist the orange and green wires together. Now you can trigger it at just the right moment.

THE PAYOFF

Suggest a round of ghost stories. When it's your turn, tell one about "The Screamer." Shine your flashlight onto your face from below to heighten the creepiness. When your friends are on the edge of their seats, say something like, "Who is that?" — and point the flashlight at the photodetector. The gadget will scream and your friends will freak.

Don't shine the flashlight anywhere near the light sensor until you're ready.

THE SCREAMER!

About five years ago, a series of bizarre murders in this neighborhood had the police stumped. The murder victims had no injuries, but their hair had turned white. They were always discovered with their eyes wide open — as if they had been scared to death.

Witnesses near every crime scene reported hearing a horrible, blood-chilling scream.

After seven murders, everything stopped. No one heard any more screams — until two nights ago, when the eighth body was found on [Insert name of local street here].

After interviewing witnesses, police concluded that the screams hadn't come from the victims — they came from the killer. The press nicknamed him The Screamer. The police were hot on the trail of The Screamer when . . . Wait . . . did you hear that? LOOK OUT!

(POINT YOUR FLASHLIGHT AT THE LIGHT SENSOR.)

AAAAAAAAAAAAGH!

GASLIGHTING
SOUND SETTING: *SCREAM*

THE SETUP

This prank is named after an old movie where a man tricks his wife into thinking she's going crazy. Hide your gadget in a dim spot in a room where your target will be. Place the photodetector where you can hit it with a small, powerful flashlight from wherever you plan to sit. Test it to make sure the flashlight activates the alarm.

THE PAYOFF

When your target is in the room, sit quietly reading a book. Without being seen, quickly shine your flashlight at the light sensor. When it screams, don't react. When the person asks, "Didn't you hear that?" look up from your book and say, "Hear what?" Wait a while, and do it again. Repeat until the target runs out of the room screaming.

THE INTERROGATOR

PHONY LIE DETECTOR
SOUND SETTING: *SAD TROMBONE*

THE SETUP

Cut two strips of aluminum foil, each about 2 feet (0.6 m) long and 1 inch wide. Tape one end of each strip to the underside of your gadget case. Set your gadget on a table, and hold the photodetector in your hand, with your thumb covering it.

THE PAYOFF

Tell people you have a state-of-the-art lie detector. Ask for a volunteer.

Have your subject sit across from you. Explain that you will ask a series of questions, and whenever the machine detects a lie, the alarm will sound. Then say, "First, I have to hook you up to it." Instruct your subject to hold a foil strip tightly in each hand.

Begin the interview with innocent questions like "What's your name?" or "Where do you live?" Then move on to potentially embarrassing ones. Whenever you want to make it look like your subject is lying, discreetly move your thumb away from the photodetector.

DO YOU EVER PICK YOUR NOSE?
HAVE YOU EVER SNOOPED IN MY ROOM?
WHAT ARE YOU GETTING ME FOR MY BIRTHDAY?

WHAT'S YOUR
WORST FEAR?
ISN'T IT
ACTUALLY. . .
BUNNIES?!

ARE YOU
LYING NOW?

HOW A REAL LIE DETECTOR WORKS

A real lie detector (called a polygraph) measures physical responses that a person doesn't have much control over: a cuff monitors your blood pressure, electric leads on your fingers detect changes in your skin, and tubes across your chest measure your breathing. When people feel anxious — as they might when lying about important stuff — a polygraph can pick up the silent signals.

POINTERS FOR PRANKSTERS

- BEFORE MOVING YOUR THUMB, MISDIRECT YOUR SUBJECT'S ATTENTION BY LOOKING INTENTLY AT THE LIE DETECTOR (YOUR GADGET).

- IF ANYONE ASKS WHY YOU'RE HOLDING ON TO THE WIRE COMING FROM THE LIE DETECTOR, SAY SOME SCIENTIFIC-SOUNDING MUMBO JUMBO ABOUT CALIBRATING THE GALVANIC SKIN RESPONSES.

- TO KEEP YOUR SUBJECT'S EYES OFF THE PHOTODETECTOR, WAVE YOUR OTHER HAND SLOWLY BACK AND FORTH. EXPLAIN THAT THIS OCCUPIES THE SUBCONSCIOUS MIND, GIVING A MORE ACCURATE READING.

MOTION SENSOR

One wrong move. . . Gotcha!

DO THIS FIRST

1. Build your basic gadget (page 5) and wire it so it's a light sensor (page 6). This light sensor can also be a motion sensor, detecting moving shadows.

2. Put the gadget in a well-lit area. Wave your hand so its shadow passes over the gadget's photodetector. The darkness of the shadow resets the gadget, then the light triggers the sound.

3. Experiment to figure out how far away your hand can be and still set off the alarm.

4. Set the gadget on a table and try to set off the alarm by walking past. If the alarm doesn't sound, check to see where your shadow is falling.

Have you ever heard a chime play when you entered a store? When you walked through the door, a motion sensor triggered the sound.

HOW DOES A SHADOW TRIP THE ALARM?

Your gadget's photodetector is an on-off switch that's controlled by light.

When you wave your hand over your gadget, the photodetector is in the shade for a moment, then back in the light. Electrons in the photodetector absorb energy from the light. Those energized electrons move in an electric current that travels through the speaker and sets off a sound.

HOW CAN AN ELECTRIC CURRENT MAKE A SOUND?

Put your hand on your throat and say, "Only the shadow knows." Feel that buzzing vibration? That's the sound of your words. Every sound starts with a vibration.

The speaker in your gadget uses two magnets to turn current into a vibration. One is an ordinary magnet that's fixed in place. The other is an electromagnet — a special magnet that only works with electricity — that's attached to a thin plastic cone.

Current flowing through the speaker controls whether the electromagnet is pulled toward the regular magnet or pushed away from it. All the pushing and pulling vibrates the plastic cone so fast that it makes the gotcha sound you can hear.

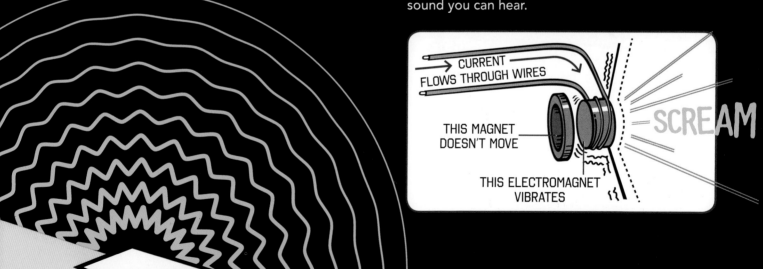

CURRENT FLOWS THROUGH WIRES

THIS MAGNET DOESN'T MOVE

THIS ELECTROMAGNET VIBRATES

SCREAM

SNEAKY STUFF

A motion sensor is a bit like a watchdog — it quietly naps until something gets too close.

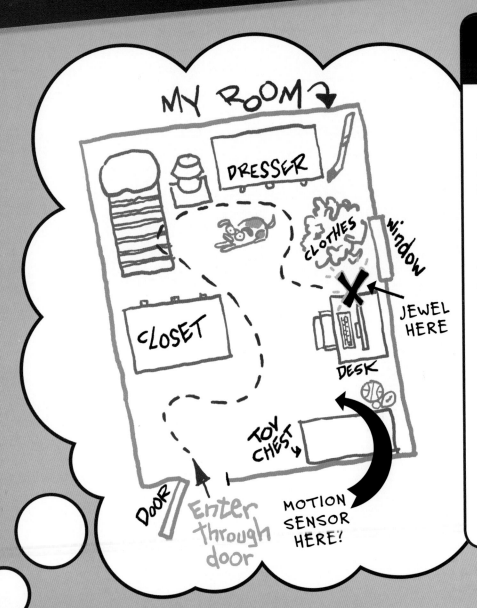

MY ROOM →

DRESSER

CLOTHES

Window

CLOSET

JEWEL HERE

DESK

TOY CHEST

DOOR

Enter through door

MOTION SENSOR HERE!

JEWEL THIEF TRAINING
SOUND SETTING: *SAD TROMBONE*

THE SETUP

Place an object — the "jewel" — in a conspicuous spot. Send your friend out of the room while you set up the gadget somewhere between the jewel and the door.

THE PAYOFF

Challenge your friend to enter the room, snatch the jewel, and make a getaway — all without triggering the alarm. If the alarm sounds, it's your turn. Leave the room while your friend repositions the alarm. Keep switching turns until one of you successfully swipes the jewel.

Good names for priceless jewels:

• The Green Gryphon
• The Eye of Time
• Stargleam

Bad names for priceless jewels:
• The Shiny Wad
• Zeus's Freckle
• Ronald

POINTERS FOR PRANKSTERS

- SET UP YOUR TRICKS IN AREAS WHERE THE PHOTODETECTOR GETS LOTS OF LIGHT.

- TAPE THE PHOTODETECTOR IN POSITION.

- ALWAYS TEST YOUR SETUP A FEW TIMES TO MAKE SURE IT WORKS WITH THE AVAILABLE LIGHT.

- FIGURE OUT HOW CLOSE YOU NEED TO BE TO TRIGGER THE ALARM.

- DON'T TAPE THE PHOTODETECTOR WHERE YOUR TARGET WILL ACTUALLY SIT ON IT, OR YOU MIGHT END UP WITH A BROKEN GADGET.

THE DINNER WRECKER
SOUND SETTING: *UNMENTIONABLE*

Tape your gadget to the bottom of your target's chair. Tape the motion sensor wire to the side of the chair so the photodetector points up. When your target sits down and blocks the light, it will release the not-so-appetizing sounds.

TIP: Practice your reaction ahead of time, so you can achieve the right mix of disgust and pity.

CROSSING THE LINE

In these tricks, your gadget acts like a foot-fault judge that lets you know if someone has "crossed the line."

HOW LOW CAN YOU GO?
SOUND SETTING: *SAD TROMBONE*

THE SETUP

Put the limbo cover on your gadget. Ask one of your friends to be the official Limbo Lord. This is a huge honor. Tape the photodetector so it points across a doorway, about 4 feet (1.2 m) off the floor. The Limbo Lord holds the gadget to support it. (Did we mention this is a huge honor?)

THE PAYOFF

Now line up your friends and have them bend backward and "dance" through the doorway. The trick is to bend below the photodetector so you don't block the light. If the sad trombone plays, that player is out. If everyone can limbo through once, the Limbo Lord moves the photodetector a little lower. When only one person can limbo under the line, that person wins.

FIRST ONE THERE'S A ROTTEN EGG

SOUND SETTING: *UNMENTIONABLE*

Invite your friends to run a race, and have your gadget set up at the finish line. Be a good sport and let someone else win the race. The runner who crosses the line first will trigger a triumphant sound effect. Way to go!

SNAP!

EGO BOOSTER

SOUND SETTING: *APPLAUSE*

Mount the gadget next to a mirror in your bedroom. Point the photodetector out, toward the spot you'll be walking past. Every time you walk by you'll receive the praise you deserve. Take a bow, blow some kisses, and get on with your day, secure in the knowledge that imaginary millions are wild about you.

PUSH BUTTON

Time for a switch!

DO THIS FIRST

1. Start with your basic gadget (page 5). Look at your gadget from the back, and untwist any wires you twisted together earlier. Make sure the metal ends of the wires aren't touching one another.

2. Take both metal switch pieces off the dock and touch them together. When you move them apart, your gadget will make a sound. Touching the pieces together resets the gadget so it's ready to sound off again.

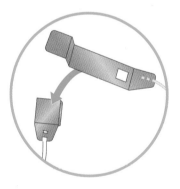

3. Slide the lower "leg" of the short metal switch piece into the orange or yellow push-button slot — it doesn't matter which. The cardboard of the dock will be pinched between the upper and lower legs. Do not cover the switch pin hole.

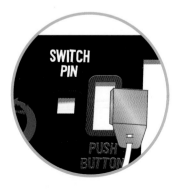

SWITCH PIN

PUSH BUTTON

4. Hold the long switch piece as shown below, set it on top of the short piece, and pin it to the dock with the switch pin. When you're done, make sure the two pieces of metal are touching.

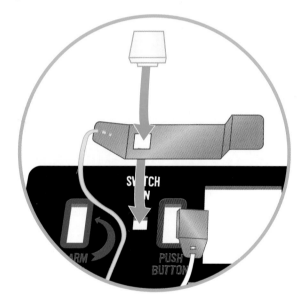

SWITCH PIN

ARM

PUSH BUTTON

5. To test your switch, turn the gadget over. Stick your finger through the hole and gently press on the long switch piece. When the pieces separate, the gadget will sound.

6. Put your gadget in a case (page 8) and add the push-button cover of your choice (page 9).

For troubleshooting tips, go to klutz.com/gotchagadgets

HOW DOES THE PUSH-BUTTON SWITCH WORK?

If an electric current is like cars driving on a highway, a switch is like a drawbridge that can block a particular road.

In your gadget, an electric current traveling through the speaker triggers a sound. When no one is pushing the button, the metal pieces are touching — making a shortcut that lets all the traffic bypass the speaker. No traffic through the speaker; no sound.

When you push the button, the metal pieces separate — opening a drawbridge on that shortcut. Because the shortcut is blocked, the cars travel through the speaker — triggering whatever sound you've chosen.

Not pushing button.

The switch pieces are touching. The shortcut is open.

Speaker

Push-button switch

IT'S ALARMING

Your push-button gadget is like a closed-circuit burglar alarm. In a closed-circuit alarm, electricity is always flowing. When a burglar breaks the flow of electricity by opening a door or window, the alarm sounds.

Pushing button.

The switch pieces aren't touching. The shortcut is closed.

Speaker

Push-button switch

LET 'EM KNOW HOW YOU REALLY FEEL

Have you been holding in your disapproval when people do things that bug you? No more! When you press the button, your gadget can tell the world how you feel.

COMEDY HECKLER
SOUND SETTING: *SAD TROMBONE*

The sad trombone sound cue is known the world over as a sign that someone is comically challenged. Whenever you hear a crummy joke, press the button.

WHEN HECKLING, IT'S GOOD TO HAVE A JOKE OF YOUR OWN READY, JUST IN CASE. HERE'S ONE, FREE OF CHARGE.

Three guys are stranded on a tropical island. They find a magic lamp and rub it. A genie comes out and says he'll grant each guy one wish. The first guy says, "I wish I was back home." Poof! It happens. The second guy says, "I wish I was back home, too." Poof! It happens. The third guy says, "I'm lonely. I wish the other two guys were here."

THE BAD HABIT BREAKER

SOUND SETTING: *SCREAM*

Do you know anyone with a bad habit they are (or should be) trying to break? Help them out. Grab your gadget and follow that person around. The second you see the bad-habit-doer doing that bad-habit thing, press the button. Then say, "You're welcome."

BAD HABITS (OTHER PEOPLE'S, THAT IS) TO BREAK WITH YOUR GOTCHA GADGET:

Fingernail biting

Gum smacking

Nose picking

Fibbing

Slouching too much

Not slouching enough

Using poor grammar

Making annoying sounds

GAME SHOW BUZZER

SOUND SETTING: *UNMENTIONABLE*

Keep the gadget nearby when you're playing games or watching game shows on TV. When someone gives an incorrect answer, accompany it with a suitable sound effect.

NOW THEY'RE PUSHIN' IT

With these activities, the gotchas are right at your fingertips.

DOORBELL

The doorbell serves two purposes: To announce you have company and to let them know they are entering the You Zone — where anyone can call the shots as long as they are you.

SOUND SETTING: *YOU CHOOSE*

Everybody has a front doorbell, but only super cool people get a doorbell where it's really needed — their room. Choose a cover, pick a sound, and hang your doorbell on the doorknob. Start screening visitors in style.

YOU MUST BE **THIS COOL** → TO ENTER THIS ROOM

NO BIG DEAL
SOUND SETTING: *SCREAM*

Conduct a (potentially profitable) experiment testing the power of advertising. Here's how: Create a cardboard case for your gadget with a hole for the button and a money slot. Make a sign that says, "Push the button to receive a screaming deal! Only $1!" Draw big arrows pointing to the push button and to the money slot. Make sure you and your gadget can make a quick getaway when your customers realize they've been hornswoggled.

OBSTACLE COURSE TIPS

- THINK LEVELS. YOU WANT OBSTACLES AT CRAWLING HEIGHT, JUMPING HEIGHT, AND CLIMBING HEIGHT.

- MAKE A BAR BY PLACING A BROOM ACROSS TWO CHAIRS. SLITHER UNDER.

- TAKE ADVANTAGE OF PRE-EXISTING OBSTACLES: BUSHES ARE GOOD HURDLES, TREES WERE MADE TO CLIMB, AND SWING SETS ARE PERFECT FOR THE SLALOM (A ZIGZAG COURSE). EVEN CRACKS IN A SIDEWALK CAN SERVE AS MUST-AVOID HAZARDS.

EXTREME OBSTACLE CHALLENGE
SOUND SETTING: *APPLAUSE*

Your gadget is the perfect endpoint for any obstacle course. The first person to complete the course presses the button and wins the applause.

DOOR ALARM

Let visitors know how welcome they aren't.

DO THIS FIRST

Stand outside your bedroom and close the door. Which side of the door is the knob closest to — the right or the left? Armed with this valuable information, you're ready to assemble your door alarm. You can set it up on any door that opens away from you.

1. Start with your basic gadget (page 5). Set the choose-a-sound switch to #4.

2. Take the large switch piece off the dock and set it aside.

3. Untwist any wires you twisted together earlier. Twist the metal ends of the orange and purple wires together. Clip the twisted ends with the alligator clip.

4. If the doorknob is on the right, move the short metal switch piece into the blue alarm slot. If your doorknob is on the left, leave it in the green slot. The open side of the switch piece will face the edge of the dock.

DOORKNOB ON RIGHT

DOORKNOB ON LEFT

5. Set the long switch piece on top of the short switch piece. The end will stick out past the edge of the dock. Your gadget will scream three times. Pin the long piece to the dock with the switch pin.

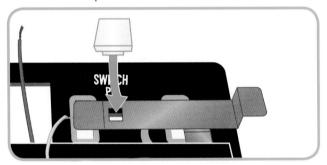

6. Add a door alarm cover (see page 9).

For troubleshooting tips, go to klutz.com/gotchagadgets

SNOOPER STOPPER
SOUND SETTING: *SCREAM*

THE SETUP

Hang the gadget over your doorknob on the outside of your room. The long switch piece sticks out past the edge of the gadget case. Position this piece between the door and the doorjamb, and gently close the door. It may take some adjusting, but when you get it right, the closing door will separate the two switch pieces.

THE PAYOFF

If somebody opens the door, the alarm will alert you. Who will shriek louder — the alarm or your sister?

ALARMING SCIENCE!

What's going on?

HOW DOES THE ALARM WORK?

Electricity flows through your gadget's speaker only when the wires and other electrical connections form a complete loop, or circuit, starting at one terminal of the battery, passing through the speaker, and returning to the other terminal of the battery.

When the end of the door alarm's long switch piece is between the door and the doorjamb, the closed door holds the two switch pieces apart. The gap between the metal pieces breaks the loop, so electricity can't flow.

When an intruder opens the door, the two metal switch pieces snap together, completing the circuit. The current flows, triggering the alarm.

The circuit board controls how many times the alarm makes your chosen sound. We figured three screams would be enough to strike terror into the heart of any trespasser.

IT'S ALARMING (AGAIN)

This type of door alarm is called an open-circuit alarm. The switch starts out open, with a space between the two pieces. When an intruder unintentionally lets the pieces snap together, that closes the switch and sets off the alarm.

Door is closed. Bridge is up. Switch pieces aren't touching. No current flows.

Speaker

Door alarm switch

Door is open. Bridge is down. Switch pieces touch. Current flows.

Speaker

Door alarm switch